BRITAIN IN PICTURES
THE BRITISH PEOPLE IN PICTURES

BRITISH GOLF

GENERAL EDITOR
W. J. TURNER

The Editor is most grateful to all those who have
so kindly helped in the selection of illustrations
especially to officials of the various public
Museums Libraries and Galleries and
to all others who have generously
allowed pictures and MSS
to be produced

BRITISH GOLF

BERNARD DARWIN

WITH
8 PLATES IN COLOUR
AND
27 ILLUSTRATIONS IN
BLACK & WHITE

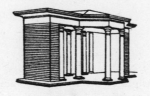

COLLINS · 14 ST. JAMES'S PLACE · LONDON

MCMXLVI

PRODUCED BY
ADPRINT LIMITED LONDON

PRINTED IN GREAT BRITAIN
BY JARROLD AND SONS LTD NORWICH
ON MELLOTEX BOOK PAPER MADE
BY TULLIS RUSSELL AND CO LTD MARKINCH SCOTLAND

LIST OF ILLUSTRATIONS

PLATES IN COLOUR

BLACK AND WHITE ILLUSTRATIONS

OLD ALICK, CADDIE AND HOLE-CUTTER
THE ROYAL BLACKHEATH GOLF CLUB
Oil painting by Mr. Gallen, c. 1835

INTRODUCTION

INNUMERABLE books have been written on golf and of those many, perhaps too many, have begun a history of the game from the earliest times or a discussion of its origin, whether Dutch or Scottish. The thing has been learnedly done to death and moreover this is to be but a short book. So such preliminary history as I shall attempt will deal only with the changes in the implements for playing the game, in particular the ball, and still more briefly with the architecture of our courses.

The evolution of clubs has been a steady, gradual and beneficent process, but as compared with that of the ball hardly a revolutionary one. No doubt that process was accentuated with the coming of the nineteenth century. We are told that to the early part of that century belongs the "civilisation of golf clubs" when the "thorn-tree" hitherto used gave way first to apple

7

and then to beech heads. Doubtless also much is due to Hugh Philip, who raised a craft to an art and whose wooden clubs, so frail and elegant, are things of true beauty. The nearest approach to a revolution was the greater use of iron clubs for approaching and the consequent if gradual atrophy of the race of spoons and baffies. This we are taught to attribute to Allan Robertson (1815–1859) and his deadly and iconoclastic wielding of the cleek in the shots up to the hole. The shortening of wooden heads, the coming of the bulger, the birth of that hybrid the mashie, all these are no more than incidents, if interesting ones. In comparatively recent times steel shafts have almost entirely superseded wooden ones. Incidentally it may be noted that steel shafts were first made and patented as long ago as 1897 by one Thomas Horsburgh, a Midlothian blacksmith, and his clubs are to be seen in the Baberton clubhouse near Edinburgh. Steel shafts were revolutionary from the club-maker's point of view but hardly from the player's. For him it made the game a little easier, as all modern developments have tended to do, but it was only a step in the evolutionary process. The same may be said of the making of graduated series of irons. It made an absurdity of the vast and clanging burdens carried by some players or rather by their caddies, unprotected by a trade union. It was so far revolutionary that it affected the hitherto untrammelled freedom of the subject by producing a mild, too mild, limitation of armaments. But it had no very notable effect on the playing of the game. To the club's history belongs no memorable and historic date.

It is otherwise with the ball. Here are at least two dates for every earnest student to remember since each marks the beginning of an epoch. They are 1848 and 1902. For untold years before 1848 the golf ball had been made of feathers tightly stuffed into a leather cover. We know on the authority of old Tom Morris that these balls "could play fine afore the wind" but they were very apt to open at the seams, particularly in wet weather, and then they were useless. They cost half a crown or at least two shillings and must have been an expensive luxury for players of limited means. In 1848 a new star arose to lighten the golfer's darkness, the star of gutta-percha. From that moment the feathery was doomed.

That was unquestionably a revolution but there was a still greater one in 1902, when the gutty was hurled from the throne it had held unchallenged for hard on fifty-four years by the rubber-cored Haskell from America. Never was there an overthrow more sudden and complete and how quickly it came I may illustrate by a mild story about myself. In May of 1902 I was setting out for the Amateur Championship at Hoylake and, having some hopes of playing for England in the first international match, I went a few days beforehand. At Euston I met a friend who said, "Are you going to play with the new American ball?" and I had never heard of it and asked what it was. The final of the Championship was between two users of the Haskell, and its fame soon spread abroad. Even as Allan Robertson had

THE FIRST LORD MACDONALD OF THE ISLES AS A BOY
WITH HIS BROTHER SIR JAMES MACDONALD OF SLEAT
Oil painting by an unknown artist of the eighteenth century

By courtesy of the Honourable Company of Edinburgh Golfers

MR. JOHN TAYLOR
CAPTAIN OF THE HONOURABLE COMPANY OF EDINBURGH GOLFERS
Oil painting by Sir John Watson Gordon

stood out against the gutty so the professionals now stood out against the rubber-core, but when one of their number, Sandy Herd, went back on his resolve and won the Open Championship with a Haskell, a fight which could in any case have had only one end was the more swiftly and irretrievably lost.

It is possible to say, not without reason, that some of the glory of golf departed for ever with the gutty ball. But it is not possible honestly to deny that the rubber-core was, through its resilient quality, a pleasanter ball to play with and this not merely because it was less exacting in point of accuracy and more merciful to the half-hit shot. The sensation of first hitting one and the sweetness with which it flew away can never fade wholly from the mind. It was perhaps a pity that the ball was ever invented but, save in the minds of a few die-hards, there never could be any question of going back. Beyond all doubt the Haskell made the game more enjoyable for the great mass of players.

I think it may be said, though the statement is a controversial one, that in the first few years of its existence the ball gave much innocent pleasure without irretrievably hurting the game. Scores grew lower but there is not necessarily any harm in that; the ball went farther but not far enough to make fools of the courses by rendering negligible many of their natural features. It was rather when golf began again after the 1914 war that the harm became apparent. The ball-makers concentrated more and more on one point, power; the new smaller and heavier ball they produced bored its way too easily through the wind and went too far. In particular some devil within its jerkin was so amenable to hard hitting that the difference between the medium and the long driver was vastly emphasised and the long hitter became so long that there remained for him hardly such a thing as a good two-shot hole. As far as he was concerned the brassy was atrophied and he reached every hole with a drive and a shot with some lofted iron. More and more lengthening, more and more space and so more and more money were wanted and even so the old balance of the game was gravely impaired.

There was no hope of reform as far as the man in the street was concerned, for he thought only of the length of his own drive. At last, however, the authoritative bodies all over the world were canvassed; their verdict was in favour of a reduction of power and the matter would have been considered at St. Andrews in September 1939 but for the war. Six years passed and with the gradual renascence ofter the war came the obvious time for doing something. What it may be is not yet known, and as I write the decision has yet again been postponed, this time for three years. That the ultimate reform, if there be one, will not be alarmingly revolutionary I can prophesy. That it will restore something of the lost balance of the game, and in particular the old glories of the second shot, I can only and most profoundly hope.

9

GULLANE
Etching by Richard Aikman after John Smart
From *Views of the Golf Greens of Scotland*, 1893

This increased power of the ball has had, of course, the effect of making courses grow ever longer, but for an historian, however modest, there are two points more important than that, the astonishing growth of courses, not in length but in number, and the arrival, not in fact but in effect, of inland golf. And both these things have happened in a little over fifty years.

Some fifty-eight years ago there was published a slender volume in a scarlet cover with gold lettering, the first number of *The Golfing Annual*. I have counted the courses in it, as well as I can, and in Scotland, the home of the game, there were then only some sixty-one, and many of those were humbly described as being rough and new. In England, then in process, in Mr. Arthur Balfour's phrase, of "Scotification," there were forty-six. Those figures are eloquent of the golf boom in living memory, and that in Scotland fully as much as elsewhere; but there is this difference to be observed. The then classical courses in Scotland remain largely the classical courses now. Muirfield it is true was not yet born and historic Musselburgh has since become a museum piece, but the broad generalisation may stand. It is very different in England. In that same number of *The Golfing Annual* Mr. Horace Hutchinson wrote of a match on the principal English greens against a certain James Macpherson, a Mrs. Harris of his own invention, and here they are: Hoylake, Westward Ho!

THE DYKE HOLE, NORTH BERWICK
Etching by Richard Aikman after John Smart
From *Views of the Golf Greens of Scotland,* 1893

Bembridge, Wimbledon, Blackheath, Felixstowe, Yarmouth, and Alnmouth. No Sandwich, it will be observed, no Deal, no Formby, no St. Anne's, no Saunton or Burnham. Blackheath is, alas! no more, and of the other seven Hoylake and Westward Ho! would certainly keep their places to-day but the rest would as certainly lose theirs.

There might well be inland courses in such a list to-day but they would all be new ones. In the 'eighties, inland golf was no more than a poor substitute for the real thing, a *pis aller,* to be played for the most part over glorified meadows of extreme muddiness. Then with the later 'nineties it was discovered that the waste country of heather and bracken, sand and fir trees would make such courses as had not been dreamed of. It took time and money but the thing could be done. Seaside golf was still the real thing *in excelsis* but there was a lesser but still real thing inland and sand was no longer the exclusive boast of links as opposed to courses.

With this rise of inland golf there came an immense upward step in the art of designing courses. With the twentieth century the golf architect came into being. Sometimes he was a professional, more often an amateur golfer. In either case he was an artist. He had gone back to the admittedly great holes of the elder courses and tried to discover the qualities which made them great. With this knowledge he became a creator. The old links

11

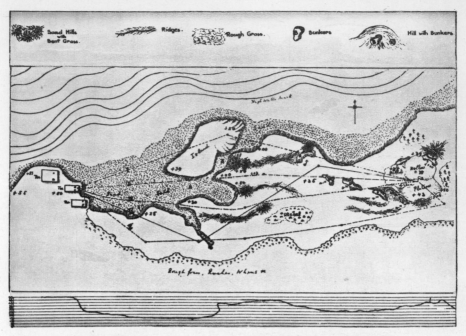

PRIZE DESIGN FOR A HOLE BY DR. A. MACKENZIE, 1914
A hole devised to make the player use his own judgment, according to his
driving powers and the weather conditions, as to which of five routes he will adopt

had grown imperceptibly into their present form, the names of their piece-
meal designers forgotten or unknown. The new inland course sprang
largely from one man's brain and became his monument.

Golf differs from almost every other game in that every piece of land on
which it is played has its own characteristics and scenery and flavour. It is
no flat, bare expanse, but is made up of miniature hills and valleys, each
with a personality of its own. A longer book than this could easily be filled
with the joys and beauties of British courses, but then a much longer book
still would not suffice for the deeds of the famous golfers who have played
over them. Rather than fall between two stools I have to make my choice,
and I choose the golfers. The play is the thing; the human interest comes
before the geographical, and with that apology I shall plunge straight ahead.

A Scottish professional once said of a famous amateur, "The only
difference that I can see between Mr. So-and-so and the professionals is that
he gets mair to eat and mair to drink." In its day that may have been a fair
distinction. The professional was with a few exceptions, little more than a

GOLF AT THE ROYAL BLACKHEATH CLUB IN 1859
Wood engraving from the *Graphic*

glorified caddie leading a rather precarious, hand-to-mouth existence. There were few courses that needed his services as a green-keeper. He might be and sometimes was a good club-maker and might thus gain steady employment, but in many cases his inclinations tended rather towards the casual than the regular. It is an illuminating fact that till the famous Bob Ferguson of Musselburgh, afterwards three times Champion, had won his first tournament he had never possessed a complete set of clubs of his own, and gained that first success with a miscellaneous pack of which several were borrowed. Moreover, whether or not the amateur had, as was suggested, more to drink, the professional was disposed to have at least as much as was good for him.

That state of things has, it is needless to say, long since been changed and the professional has been for years the respected and self-respecting member of society that we know to-day. The amateur has changed too in that he has now as a rule to work for his living and cannot give so much time to the game as he once could. That anonymous amateur of the aphorism could presumably play golf to his heart's content, could play it at least as often as any professional. If we scan the list of the amateurs who first became famous figures in the game we find for the most part that they were so fortunately situated as to have a great deal of leisure. They might have some business or profession but it was seldom of a very exacting character. They might have other interests and amusements besides golf, witness Young Tommy Morris's bitter cry as to Mr. Gilbert Mitchell Innes: "I cannot understand Mr. Innes, when he's playing as fine a game as ony mortal man ever played, leaving gowf to rin after a wheen stinking beasts, and then comin' back, no able to hit a ba'." The distinguished amateur might be guilty of such a lamentable desertion of the links but it was his deliberate act; he could generally play as much golf as he wanted. Those so happily circumstanced have grown fewer as time has gone on and it is not hard to prophesy that, in golf as in first-class cricket, they will in the post-war world grow fewer still.

Leaving on one side these social phenomena there will always be this difference between the professional and the amateur, that the professional is the better player. Every now and again there may arise a John Ball, a Hilton or a Bobby Jones, but generally the professional will excel the amateur as he does in other walks of life, just because he is a professional and the game is his means of livelihood. That is the great and abiding distinction between the two classes. I shall therefore adopt the same division as did Mr. Everard in that chapter in the *Badminton* over which I pored in boyhood, on "Some Celebrated Players."

GOLF MATCH BETWEEN LONDON SCOTTISH CLUBS AND BLACKHEATH AT WIMBLEDON, 1870
Wood engraving from the *Graphic*

PROFESSIONALS

BY this time there have been so many professionals of just celebrity that I must divide them into epochs or ages, giving a few words to the leaders in each epoch. In every game there is what may be called an heroic age. These ages may differ in point of actual date according to the antiquity of the game or the time at which the players first found a *vates sacer*, but they are alike in this, that the memory of game-playing man goes no farther back. In cricket the heroic age is clearly that of the Hambledon Club and its great players as recorded by John Nyren, which may be roughly said to extend from 1780 to 1820. There is a corresponding age in golf which, though later in date, possesses much the same romantic quality and the same legendary figures and may also be given a space of forty years, from 1835 to 1875. I have chosen those dates because in 1835 Allan Robertson was twenty and may be presumed to have been entering his kingdom; further, because in 1875 there died the unquestionably greatest golfer of the heroic age and as far as such comparisons are possible, one of the very greatest that ever lived, Young Tommy Morris.

15

Allan Robertson was the first outstanding golfer of whom we have any real knowledge. He was a product of the "feathery" age but, after fighting the innovation tooth and nail, remained a famous player with the gutty. Allan was a truly remarkable golfer, wonderfully skilful and accomplished, but I am wholly unable to accept the view of his contemporary admirers who put him on an unattainable pinnacle. He lacked the power which even then was beginning to tell its inevitable tale. It is said that he was never beaten, but it seems clear that he safeguarded that record by refusing to meet at least two formidable challengers, "Old" Willie Park and "Old" Tom Morris. He remained, as I judge, unbeaten much as did Kenfield, a corresponding figure in the heroic age of billiards, by refusing to meet John Roberts the elder. To me Old Tom's verdict seems as far as may be conclusive, "I could cope with Allan masel' but never wi' Tommy."

True, that was an illustrious father's verdict on a still more illustrious son and may possibly be partial on that account, but I hardly think so. It is always a little puzzling to the modern student that Tommy the son died in 1875 and Tom the father survived till 1908. Tommy, as far as we can now recreate him from the words of those who saw him, had everything; power and dash in the long game, a deadly short game, and a quality of brilliance that could produce the extraordinarily good shot when, either owing to the lie of the ball or the state of the match, it was desperately needed.

In so far as it is either possible or profitable to compare him with his successors I can only quote the late Mr. Leslie Balfour Melville who had often played with him: "I can't imagine anyone playing better than Tommy did." As to his contemporaries, figures are eloquent. Three times running he won the Championship Belt at Prestwick and on the average he was in those three years nine strokes ahead of the second man in thirty-six holes. Then when, after a year's interval, the Cup was instituted in place of the Belt that had become his own, he won again. There was, we are told, one who could more or less hold him in an ordinary game, his friend and rival David Strath, but when it came to the point there is that average of nine strokes in two rounds, as to which there is no arguing. Some of his scores appear high to-day and there we come up against the difficulty and the futility of comparisons. Courses have grown at once harder and easier; harder from their much increased length, easier since they are less narrow and far better kept. Clubs and balls, especially balls, may not have made a better game but have given the player a power of which he would once never have dreamed. Yet there is one score of Tommy's which we can come near to appreciating at its right worth. In 1870 he won the Belt at Prestwick with 149 for the three rounds of twelve holes. Good judges who knew the links well in those days estimate the par for the twelve holes at 49. Therefore Tommy's score was only two over par for thirty-six holes, and that is a score up to a very high modern standard, achieved under conditions obviously more difficult than those of to-day. One swallow

16

ALLAN ROBERTSON AND TOM MORRIS
Wash drawing by T. Hodge, 1889

does not make a summer but that one score does show in terms that we can understand the game that this then unapproached genius could play, and with that I will leave him. He died in 1875 and those who gaze on his tombstone at St. Andrews to-day can see, or at least fancy, that the sculptor who made it caught something of the dash and fire and glorious confidence of his style.

Our next epoch is in point of years a comparatively short one. It lasts only for nineteen years, until the winning of his first Championship by an English professional, J. H. Taylor in 1894, and with him the beginning of the reign of the Triumvirate. Though brief in point of years it is historically a full one, for it saw the great golfing boom of the 'eighties, the awakening of England to the game and, at first at the hands of the amateurs rather than the professionals, the gauntlet definitely thrown down to Scotland. To it belong the names of a number of celebrated professionals, but none perhaps so definitely outstanding as those that came before or after it. There came first of all two, both now a little shadowy, each of whom won three

17

Championships in succession, Jamie Anderson of St. Andrews and Bob Ferguson of Musselburgh. Anderson I take to have been a player formed on the lines of Allan Robertson, of an accuracy that has perhaps never been excelled, but rather lacking in power. A casual remark of his own, recorded by Mr. Everard, gives a clue to his game; he said he had just finished five rounds without a single shot played otherwise than he had intended. It is no wonder that, with the heroic Tommy gone to his place, such heart-breaking blamelessness could afford to be outdriven and yet win. But Bob Ferguson sounds to me the more formidable golfer, having the power that Anderson lacked and did not try to cultivate, especially with iron clubs. He was a master of that great though now atrophied club the cleek and had once played and won a match against Young Tom in which each was armed with a cleek alone. To read of such a match is like reading of the old single-wicket matches at cricket and to wish that in these more sophisticated days there was time for such single combats. I would give many days of the boredom of scoring tournaments, of the so-called "big golf" for news-paper prizes, for one crowded hour of that match, so unmechanical, so full of variety and improvisation.

Three times Bob Ferguson won, and a fourth victory seemed to be almost in his hands when he was playing off the tie against Willie Fernie on his own Musselburgh for the Championship of 1883. With one hole to play he led by a stroke and that one hole was within comfortable reach from the tee. It was not to be, however, for he took four to the hole and Fernie holed a very long putt for two. From that point Bob Ferguson fades out of the picture, his decline accelerated by a severe illness: he gradually relapsed into the caddie from which he emerged.

Willie Fernie, whom I saw with my own eyes—he was my earliest hero when I played as a tiny boy at Felixstowe—was a beautiful, easy and graceful golfer, with an air of almost insolent confidence. I see him very plainly coming out of his shop by the Martello tower (a little paradise of pitch and cobbler's wax and divine scents), a white apron round his waist, a shiny-peaked yachting cap set rakishly on his head, in his hand a half-finished driver which he waggles lovingly and knowingly. There are others too in this age that many will remember; there is Archie Simpson, a glorious driver with a glorious swing; there is Willie Campbell, tough and dashing, a great player of money matches. He had one Championship in the hollow of his hand and threw it away in a single and fatal bunker in the "Loop" at Prestwick. When all was over he and his caddie sat down and wept together, as I have been told by one illustrious veteran who witnessed the sad scene.

There was Willie Park, of the great Musselburgh family, who practised putting on a tiled floor till his back ached, and became perhaps the deadliest putter that ever lived. Park was a great player and that though he struggled all his life against a certain raggedness in his long game; he never

18

A Caddie to the "Royal and Ancient"
Coloured etching by J. Doby after W. D. Sadler, 1914

attained to anything like that mechanical certainty of driving which has marked a later generation. His putting often and often pulled him through; he won two Championships; he had a rather short putt to tie with Harry Vardon for a third and missed it. All that could be done without really fine driving he did and more, but there are limits to what pluck and putting can achieve, and when he challenged Vardon to their famous match he was crushed by sheer power and accuracy of hitting. Willie Park was a remarkable man. Not for him the old hand-to-mouth, happy-go-lucky standards of his profession. He had a large and successful club-making business with a London shop; he was a thoughtful golf architect, in an altogether different class to those who had pegged out greens and built rampart bunkers by rule of thumb. He had his own golf course at Huntercombe and though this

19

was not, I fear, a prosperous speculation for him, he has left it in other hands as a pleasant monument to his skill. He was a notable and outstanding personage.

So, though in quite another way, was one of his contemporaries and rivals, Andrew Kirkaldy. His younger brother Hugh, whose loose, slashing swing is familiar on the back of the *Badminton* volume, was, I suppose. the more brilliant golfer, but Hugh died young whereas Andrew survived to be an old man, a monumental figure of St. Andrews and a legend in his own lifetime. Andrew was a fine and formidable golfer, with a swing which was in his day deemed a short one but now would approximate to orthodoxy, great strength and a clean decisiveness of iron play "like the shutting of a clasp knife." He was always a match player, rather than a score player. His shout as he became dormy two on Andrew Scott at the corner of the Dyke has passed into history: "The door's locked now." It is typical of that rich vein of personal hostility which by comparison wastes its sweetness in score play. Above everything else Andrew was a "character" and famous as such, but many who did not know him and have only heard his sayings have to my mind misconceived him. He had a gift of trenchant and dramatic speech but he was not a wit. He was rather a forceful and serious person who said in deadly earnest that which was reported as a witticism. He was a rough somewhat overbearing man, essentially of the old school, at once envious and contemptuous of the new, and certainly no courtier; but he had a certain natural dignity and a brusque and likeable flavour that was all his own.

Another "character" was Ben Sayers, who was to North Berwick what Andrew was to his native St. Andrews. In intense keenness, in the hostility towards the enemy which is to-day more discreetly masked, in a knowledge of all the best ways of winning a match, there was some resemblance between them; but in other ways they were very different. Andrew was big and burly; Ben a little creature, though lithe and wiry, always suggesting the acrobat of his boyhood's years; he had to make up by artifice for the power that Nature had denied him, so that the long clubs he wielded brought to mind the tail wagging the dog. There was about Ben a certain serpentine guile that Andrew did not possess; he had a keen interest in the technique of the game which made him a good coach and a businesslike shrewdness which, combined with a genuine enthusiasm, could wile a bird off a bush in the matter of selling clubs. A wonderful player for his size was Ben and of a lion's heart as a match player. "Give me a wind," he said once before a Championship at Muirfield, "and I'll show you who'll be Champion," but that favouring wind never blew for him.

I have kept to the last one who was never Champion but who was in my belief the greatest player of all the professionals of this period, Douglas Rolland. Alas! that I never saw him save as an older man crippled with rheumatism and I can only judge from his rather fragmentary achievements

A Stymie: Musselburgh
Heliogravure after an oil painting by J. C. Dollman, 1899

and from all I have gathered from those who knew him. On one point there is, I think, very general agreement, namely that in point of combined length and accuracy he was the finest driver that ever hit a gutty ball. He was a magnificent figure of a man, strikingly handsome as his pictures show, with a glorious swing and an innocent happiness in his own powers. "Awa' she sails wi' dash and spray" he would exclaim as the ball sped away. Mr. Harry Colt who often played with him is my authority for this pleasant story, reminiscent of Alan Breck's "Am I no a bonny fighter?" By comparison with his driving his shorter iron shots and putting were almost crude, a merciful provision of nature that prevented him from being invincible.

Another point on which all are agreed was his lovableness as a man. He seems to have been one of those to whom the hackneyed phrase was really applicable, that he was no one's enemy but his own. The two traditional pitfalls in the path of mankind were something too much for him, and having got a job in England he thought it wisest for diplomatic reasons never to play in Scotland, a fact which greatly limited his Championship activities. He had a happy-go-lucky way of appearing at the last moment to play a match with no clubs of his own, only to borrow a miscellaneous set and beat the record. He was by all accounts the most incorrigibly casual and delightful person, doubtless a bad example but a tremendous golfer.

21

J. H. TAYLOR
Finish of a full drive

Even under the severe limitations which hampered his career, his record is a striking one. It began in 1883 when some Hoylake admirers of Mr. John Ball (not yet arrived at his full stature but a very fine player) issued on his behalf a challenge to play any amateur. Rolland accepted it and gained so great a lead over his own course at Elie that the second half at Hoylake could be little more than a procession. This, one would think, would have caused some stir, but it apparently roused no misgivings in the following summer at St. Andrews when there came a message asking if anyone would give a match to two stonemasons from Elie. Mr. Horace Hutchinson and Mr. Leslie Balfour said they would. The two stonemasons arrived; their names were Rolland and Simpson and their adversaries had never heard of them. They seemed, as Mr. Hutchinson later wrote, two very nice young men, but presently, in his words, they got their hammers really to work and then they seemed rather less agreeable, for they drove incredible distances and severely chastised their distinguished hosts. A little later there came a comforting circumstance. The Open Championship was played at Prestwick and Mr. Hutchinson read the result: Jack Simpson first, Douglas Rolland second.

The Championship knew him not again, I think, till it was played for the first time in England at Sandwich in 1894. He played well but not quite well enough, for this was the year of Taylor's first victory (my epochs must overlap now and again) and Rolland was second five strokes behind him. In the Amateur and Professional tournament that followed he had a measure of revenge beating the new Champion in the final by 2 and 1. That was in effect the end of his career, although he was only thirty-four; his health failed and he faded out of the picture. Of all the players that I could wish to have seen I put Rolland first, bracketed with

Young Tom. There seems to me no more romantic figure in the story of golf.

That match between Rolland and Taylor really belongs to my third epoch, the epoch of the Triumvirate, from 1894 to 1914. There can be no doubt as to the justification of the title. During those years those three men, Taylor, Vardon and Braid, won the Open Championship sixteen times between them and five other men managed to win it once each. I think the epoch should strictly be ante-dated by one year to 1893 when Taylor paid his first visit to Scotland to play in the Championship at Prestwick. He did not win or even nearly win; victory went to Willie Auchterlomie, a very fine golfer, now a beloved monument at St. Andrews as the professional to the Royal and Ancient Club. During a week's practice all the best players of the day flung themselves one after another at Taylor's head and sank back beaten. When the Championship began he started with an almost incredibly good round of 75; then collapsed with a second round of 89 and finished in the end tenth. But he had done enough to show that a new star had arisen so bright that it could not possibly be dimmed for long.

Taylor drove straighter than the others, he put his approaches nearer the hole and he putted well enough. Here was a combination of qualities that must win and demanded a higher standard of golf from anyone who meant to hold his own with the new prodigy. Yet though the coming of Taylor synchronised with a definite improvement in golf, it may be questioned whether he was wholly responsible for it. That in which he clearly excelled was in the bold and accurate playing of shots of whatever length to the green. There was no more question of a cleek for safety when the young man from Winchester was hitting brassy shots right up to the pin. He was bolder and more accurate than any of his forerunners, but this new school of golf had perhaps been founded a little earlier and that by an amateur, John

JAMES BRAID
Finish of a mashie shot

23

Ball. Mr. Ball had won his Open Championship three years before and I know that in Mr. Hilton's view it was he who had first opened the eyes of golfers to what could be done in the matter of this direct attack on the pin, once it was within reach with any club.

At any rate in the next year when Taylor became Champion his type of game was widely seen and revealed to many people new possibilities of the far and the sure combined. It is a commonplace in every kind of game and sport that where one man shows the way to hitherto unscaled heights others are forced to follow him and so it was now. For two years or so Herd, already well known before Taylor's coming, was his chief rival, a truly grand golfer who could fully hold his own in matches, but under the long-drawn-out strain of the Championship was a little apt to fade. It would be unfair to say of him that he went up like a rocket and came down like the stick, but he had something too much of the excitable and poetic temperament that hears the joy bells ringing before victory is won; he lacked nothing of the bravery but something of the dogged lasting power of the English player. It was not that Taylor had not what is to-day called "temperament." He could plumb abysms of woe as he could reach heights of ecstasy, but in either case he had a power of clenching his teeth and controlling the passing mood such as is given to few. Like Bobby Jones after him he could make of sometimes unruly emotions his servants instead of his masters.

In 1894 and 1895 Taylor called the tune to which others must learn to dance. There soon appeared two apt learners and it chanced that in each case it was Taylor himself who assisted at his rival's début. In 1895 he played an exhibition match on the West Drayton course, some sad be-bungalowed remnants of which can still be seen from a railway carriage window, against one James Braid. There were rumours of a club-maker at the Army and Navy Stores who was a very fine player, but to the general public he was unknown. The dark horse holed a long putt for a three to halve with the Champion and became a dark horse no longer. He had not quite arrived yet; he had not yet learned the art of putting which was so bountifully to be vouchsafed to him later; but there was no doubt of his quality. A year later Taylor went up to Ganton in Yorkshire to meet Harry Vardon, a young man who had played creditably in the Championship but no more, and had a curious unorthodox lift in his backward swing not at first sight inspiring confidence. Taylor had not played many holes of that match before he realised what he was up against and he retired beaten 8 and 7. In that same year Taylor and Vardon tied for the Championship at Muirfield and on playing off Vardon won.

With him we come to a figure as to whom we may adopt Mr. Balfour Melville's words as to Young Tom and say that it is impossible to imagine anyone playing better than he did. He did not win again in 1897 but after

WILLIAM GUNN (" CADDIE WILLIE ") AT BRUNTSFIELD LINKS, NEAR EDINBURGH
Oil painting by an unknown artist, 1839

ON MUSSELBURGH LINKS
Oil painting by Charles Lees, 1859

By courtesy of the Honourable Company of Edinburgh Golfers

that he attained for a while such a position of supremacy as no other British golfer has quite touched.

Vardon definitely set up a new and higher standard just as Taylor had done. To the same accuracy he added something more of power which put him for a little while in one class with all the other golfers in another. He could reach with two wooden-club shots greens which asked for two shots and then a pitch from nearly all the rest, and his brassy shot was likely to end as near the pin as did their pitches. Moreover though after his serious illness some years later he became famous for missing short putts, he did not miss them in his prime and a good approach putter he always was. So for a while he went up and down the country trampling down all opposition and the Championship was deemed almost as good as over before it began.

Then in 1900 he went to America to continue his triumphs, and in his own opinion he left a little of his best game there. No doubt he had forced his rivals to get just a little more out of themselves than they had deemed possible, but apart from that something of the overwhelming brilliance had gone. The golfing empire was divided. Taylor won a second time on St. Andrews. Braid came into his own at Muirfield in 1901. Herd won his solitary victory, not enough for his deserts, in 1902. Vardon reasserted himself magnificently at Prestwick in 1905 though he felt so ill during his last round that he several times thought he would not be able to finish.

He was in fact very ill and had to vanish for a while. And then Braid really began. In six years his victorious career was only twice interrupted, once by that *beau sabreur* from the Basque country of great game players, that formidable, humorous, picturesque figure, Arnaud Massy, and once by Taylor, who was always bobbing up again. Braid had always been an extremely long driver and an extremely accurate one save for a very occasional hook. He was a grand iron player, and a versatile one wedded neither to the pitch nor the run, and his strength gave him unequalled powers of recovery. In point of temperament he combined an immense tranquillity with a fire and dash which made him of set purpose go out for everything, now and again to the agony of his supporters. Now to all these gifts was added that of putting. He had once been prone to lapses on the green, to putt, in his own words, "like an auld sweetie wife." He put away such weaknesses with his putting cleek, and with an aluminium club and a slow smooth delivery he became a great putter. Perhaps he did not wholly overcome his fear of the very short ones, but during his reign he holed more middle-length putts than any other man.

At last his reign ended and our era has now nearly ended too, but its last four years brought fresh honours to its leading figures. In only one year, 1912, did one or other of them fail to win. In 1911 Vardon after a long interval came back to tie with Massy and crush him on playing off. 1912 was the year of Ray, whom old Nyren might have called, as he did

Tom Walker, "that anointed clod-stumper." With rough-hewn strength, something of a bucolic air, and a swing unpolished and unorthodox but having the saving grace of rhythm, Ray combined a delicate touch in the short game. He was unquestionably the player of his year and always a formidable one, not to be judged by any too nice and pedantic standards. Then in 1913 and 1914 came the final blaze of the Triumvirate. In 1913 at Hoylake Taylor won by almost innumerable strokes, in perhaps the vilest weather I ever saw. In 1914 at Prestwick he and Vardon leading the field were drawn together on the last day and beset by an almost intolerable rabble of spectators. After a thrilling struggle and an historic disaster for Taylor at the Pow Burn, Vardon won and took the lead for ever from his two competitors, six wins to five each of theirs. Then came the five blank war years and they took their inevitable toll. All three men played fine golf after the war but their sun was now gloriously set.

HARRY VARDON
Negotiating a stymie

After the long gap of the war golf began again with new leaders. They were not new in the sense that they had been only boys before the war; they did not burst suddenly on the world as did Tolley and Wethered among the amateurs. They were rather as are schoolboys who have been in the fifth form at the end of the summer term and come back after the holidays in September to find that the old gods of the sixth form have left and they have stepped into their once almost incredible eminence.

Duncan and Mitchell were now beyond question our two outstanding figures and well worthy as players to succeed their illustrious predecessors. Duncan was the supreme artist, with the advantages and disadvantages of the artistic temperament, capable of being sometimes wayward

26

ST. ANDREWS
Approaching the sixteenth green

and sometimes bored, but also capable of a brilliance which has never been surpassed or perhaps equalled, at any rate in this country. Mitchell was rather the craftsman than the artist but a craftsman of the very best, gifted with immense strength, a natural gift and a power of hard work which had added polish and control to the rather rough-hewn game of his amateur days. These two were both magnificent players but each lacked a little something of the determined character of their predecessors. Duncan had to be in the mood to be at his sparkling best and had not the power of making dogged resolve serve instead of inspiration. Mitchell was by nature a peaceful creature to whom the crowd and excitement of Championships brought little joy of battle; he could and did fight hard but, I think, it went against the grain with him. And so in the end Duncan won one Championship and Mitchell won none and their joint record will not tell the historian of the future what golfers they were.

For a little while we did not dream that either of the two could or would be dethroned by anyone from across the Atlantic. Nor did the first appearance of Hagen and Barnes at Deal do anything to unsettle this national complacency, for though Barnes was sixth he had not looked really dangerous, and Hagen finished far down the list. Then came St. Andrews where Jock Hutchison, once a Scot but then an American, pitching marvellously on the fast greens with his "punched" irons, tied with Mr. Wethered and won the play-off, and another American, Tom Kerrigan, came next. And after that the deluge—or rather very nearly that. Hagen won in 1922 and then Havers beat him at Troon, playing very finely, and we flattered ourselves that the rot had been stopped. Far from it, however, for Havers, a player of perhaps rather too unambitious and easy-going temperament, could not quite do it again and for ten long years nobody could do it either. Hagen, Barnes, Jones, Jones, Hagen, Hagen, Jones, Armour, Sarazen, Shute—that in the shortest possible form is the history of those depressing years in which our Cup made a formal visit here every summer to return to America by the next boat.

This book is on British golf and therefore it is not for me to enlarge on those visiting conquerors or I might write for ever. They were very, very good; there could be no sort of doubt about that; they were in particular better putters with sounder methods than were our men, and they seemed to have the priceless gift of rising to the occasion. It was not that we had not got good players for we certainly had; it seemed that they could play as well as anybody, except alas! when they most wanted to. In the Ryder Cup matches in this country they fully held their own and, though the Americans doubtless kept their eyes fixed on the supreme goal of the Championship and took care not to reach "the peak" too soon, they tried hard enough in those matches. The Ryder Cup results were encouraging and so was Compston's unexampled victory over a rather casual and untrained Hagen; but when it came to the test of the Championship it was always the same story and the more buoyant we were beforehand the heavier our fall. Finally in 1933 we won the Ryder Cup match and Shute and Craig Wood tied for the Championship, at St. Andrews of all places, and if they had not won Diegel would have won, and Sarazen most certainly ought to have won. Our eclipse was complete.

By this time perhaps familiarity had bred a little contempt and our Championship did not seem quite so glittering a prize to American invaders as it had once done. For a little while they did not come in such numbers as they had done, but if our men had by comparison a little breathing-space they used it well. When in 1937 the Americans came again in greater strength than ever before they won the Ryder Cup, but as far as the Championship was concerned they were "withered and strown" in the wind and rain of Carnoustie. Beyond any doubt our professional golf took an upward turn, alike in skill and in confidence, from 1934. Cotton, Perry, Padgham, Cotton, R. A. Whitcombe, Burton—those were the six English winners from that year of the tide's turning, and it was right and proper that the man who set the example, who won twice and won, moreover, in the year of most formidable invasion should be the most remarkable figure in this last epoch, Henry Cotton. Cotton is of course a man altogether out

HENRY COTTON
Oil painting by J. A. A. Berrie

of the ordinary run, who by shrewdness and indomitable work has at once turned himself into a magnificent golfing machine and an extremely efficient and successful business machine. In every way he has "kept his light a-shining a little in front of the rest" and made himself in his own line a unique public figure. He has not pleased everybody in doing so, but he has had the strength of mind to go on his appointed way and he has attained his end.

With the great new golfing public that has arisen in the last ten years or so his name stands for golf in a way for which there has been no parallel. Cotton's two Championship victories have been in some ways the

AN EARLY MATCH BETWEEN OXFORD AND CAMBRIDGE AT HOYLAKE
R. H. Jobson (Oxford) approaching the tenth

converse of each other. In his first at Sandwich he began with such almost inconceivable brilliancy that it seemed that nobody could get within ten strokes of him. Then having the prize in the hollow of his hand he frittered and frittered away his lead till almost anything might have happened, and then taking himself resolutely by the scruff of the neck he finished well to win with a measure of comfort. At Carnoustie he was always there or thereabouts until the last round, when he knew what he had to do to beat Whitcombe and he finished with one of the longest and finest spurts in the vilest weather that ever was seen. Since the war he has been a little fanciful and sometimes disappointing in his public appearances but I do not think anyone can doubt that given a severe and arduous test he is our best golfer.

All the other four who have won after 1934 have been well deserving of their honours and Padgham in 1936 had an *annus mirabilis* such as perhaps only Harry Vardon and Braid in their best years have equalled. He won so many tournaments and holed so many putts that when it came to the

ROYAL ST. GEORGES, SANDWICH
The bunker before the fourth green

Championship at Hoylake it seemed that he must have had his ration of both, but if the notion occurred to him he did not let it trouble him. He played with that calmness and ease, alike of temperament and swing, which made an elder generation think that Harry Vardon had come again, and he won after a desperate fight with a great last round.

I am writing at a time of transition when it is hard to say what the future may bring forth. Seven years have made nobody younger. Some of the leading pre-war figures ought to have another Championship or tw, in them but for others the time is, I fear, almost past. We shall know more when there is a whole summer of play and another American invasion. "It's aye the putting" has often been quoted and it may be quoted again. I doubt if our players have yet attained to American standards on the green but I am fairly sure that those ten years in the wilderness brought home to them a lesson which they had not fully appreciated before and by which they have profited, namely that putting is an art and not an inspiration.

31

WHEN I come to the amateurs I hardly deem it necessary to dive quite so far back. The foundation of the Amateur Championship in the middle 'eighties makes a natural starting-point and, moreover, I am modern enough to believe that the standard of amateur golf rose perceptibly with the coming of Mr. John Ball. Nevertheless there were fine players before his day and respect and romance alike demand some mention of them.

Before the time of Championships the place to look for illustrious names is in the list of winners of the Autumn Medal at St. Andrews and in the 'fifties there come three close together—Robert (later Sir Robert) Hay, James Campbell Stewart and George Glennie. Sir Robert Hay had played for insurgent youth against enthroned old age in a famous foursome, and in a single, had won his money and sent the poor old gentlemen to the right-about. He remained a fine player till he was old himself, and a great wielder of the baffy of his younger days. Mr. Glennie's fame rests securely on the fact that his record for the Autumn Medal endured for hard on thirty years, till Horace Hutchinson beat it. He was steady and accurate rather than forceful and brilliant, but unquestionably a good golfer and a great figure in the game. But my own romantic intuitions are all for that dashing young officer Lieutenant (later Captain) J. C. Stewart of the 72nd Highlanders. Pleasant legends cluster round his name; how he disdained a tee and would throw his ball down on the teeing-ground with a noble gesture and drive it from where it lay; how he dared to play Allan Robertson on level terms and held his own; how Mr. Sutherland exclaimed in agonised tones that it was "a shame of a man with such powers to go to India." I have more solid ground too for my preference. In 1853 he won the medal with 90 and before that year only two winners had scraped round under 100 with a single stroke to spare. Four years later there was held at St. Andrews what was called "The First Golf Tournament," open to pairs from all golf clubs, for the prize of a silver claret jug. Eleven clubs were represented, ten from Scotland and one from England, the Royal Blackheath. The Blackheath pair were Captain Stewart and George Glennie; they went through the field like a devouring flame and Blackheath made them life members for "Constituting this Club the Champion Golf Club of the World." I am sure Mr. Glennie did his full share, but for me Captain Stewart will always remain the heroic figure. They used to lay two to one on Allan against him. I should incontinently have taken the bet.

Another distinguished figure of those early days was Gordon McPherson, who as the Rev. J. G. McPherson, D.D., a rather complacent and self-satisfied old gentleman, lived to write a book of memoirs in which he

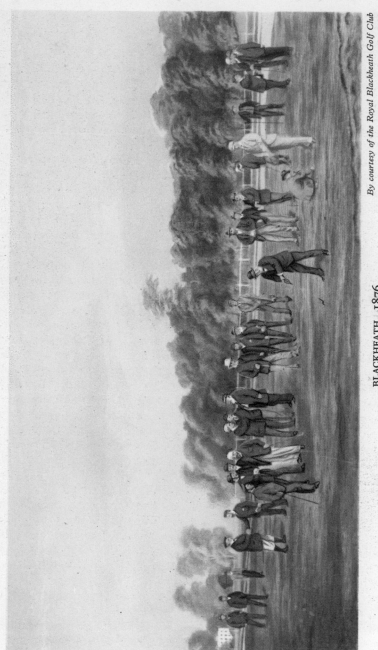

BLACKHEATH, 1876
Oil painting by F. P. Halikins

JOHN BALL
Oil painting by R. E. Morrison, 1899

praised Allan to the skies and thought rather poorly of those that came later. He is irritating but he is also interesting and beyond all doubt he was in his time as a St. Andrews student a very fine player and in particular a fine driver, capable of holding his own in professional company and with a record of 80 to his credit. I dare say he was quite as good as he thought he was.

Finally in the 'seventies there is another exciting player, Mr. Gilbert Mitchell Innes, the author of the *mot* that the way to beat a professional is never to let him get a hole up. He is of particular interest because he is one of the few who, like Mr. Walter Travis, Mr. Charles Hutchings and Mr. Sidney Fry in later times, have attained to the first rank without the advantages of a golfing boyhood. He ripened slowly but surely. He began the game at twenty-three or twenty-four; ten years later he devoted himself to it seriously; ten years later again when he was in his forties he reached his mature excellence. It was then that he played, as we are told, six hundred holes with Young Tommy as his partner against Davie Strath and Jamie Anderson, and if at the end of that long-drawn struggle he and his partner were two matches down they were eight holes up. Nobody but a really good player could thus have played his part in such company.

And so to the 'eighties when the first Amateur Championship at Hoylake makes a natural jumping-off place for a new epoch. It was a time of fierce antagonisms, and perhaps some jealousies, in which the few outstanding figures met more often than in later years. The small first class contained perhaps seven or eight players, John Ball, Horace Hutchinson, J. E. Laidlay, Leslie Balfour (afterwards Balfour Melville), Alexander Stuart, A. F. Macfie, and F. A. Fairlie. Within that again was a more select class, Ball, Hutchinson, and Laidlay, and of those three again there was one unquestionably the best, John Ball. After three unsuccessful attempts, when his adoring supporters at Hoylake were wringing their hands in despair, he won his first Championship at the age of twenty-five in 1888; he won his eighth and last in 1910 and during all those years he would have been, in John Nyren's words, "the first to be chosen of any man in England." He had great rivals and short periods of comparative and partial eclipse, but he was day in and day out, as he is still deemed by all who remember him, the greatest British amateur.

He had a swing more true and graceful than anyone can conceive who did not see him. He was a magnificent player of all kinds of iron shots, with an unequalled power of control over the swing of the club; he had immense resource in recovery, and a fine, dogged, hostile spirit which made him rise to the occasion. He could, at any rate as he grew older, be rather an indolent player till he was roused, and seemed almost to prefer the close fighting finish to the comfortable victory which he might have bestirred himself earlier to win. At the same time he had always a valuable touch of venom in his game for those whose blood he wanted. Apart from that occasional

33

laziness at the start he had but one vulnerable spot; he was apt to miss a short putt or two, and it was through that amiable weakness that his contemporaries managed sometimes to hold and beat him.

No other amateur, I might almost say no other golfer, has excited such frantic hero-worship as John Ball did at Hoylake. He said little, but his few remarks, in which he had the knack of hitting the nail on the head, were remembered and quoted. He was a shy, retiring man who shunned publicity, and the crowd followed wherever he went. There was a quality of genius in his game and perhaps in some obscure, indefinable way in the man himself, that put him on a pinnacle which no other amateur in this country has ever attained. He became a legend in his lifetime and the legend will long survive his death.

His two great contemporary opponents Horace Hutchinson and John Ernest Laidlay were both very fine players of strongly marked styles and characteristics. Horace was so noteworthy a figure as a pioneer of golf that people are apt to forget his achievements as a player. Gifted with a style dashing and flamboyant rather than orthodox, which he innocently preached in his books possibly to the detriment of his disciples, he was the master of every kind of difficult shot. He could sometimes miss the easy ones, but there was scarcely any place so bad but that his ingenuity could find a way out, and he could consummate a heart-breaking recovery by a deadly putt. From early life he was handicapped by bad health, but well and in the mood he was one of the great golfers. Horace was, by the way, the first of a long line of distinguished golfers from Oxford and Cambridge, since

HORACE HUTCHINSON
Top of swing with driver

he played for Oxford in the first University match on Wimbledon Common in 1878. In those days he and Mr. Alexander Stewart were head and shoulder above the average University player who was indeed rather an elementary person; but since the beginning of this century or perhaps it may be said since the foundation of the Oxford and Cambridge Golfing Society in 1899 there have always been some University players in the forefront of amateur golf.

Laidlay was a great golfer too in a style of his own with the ball far in front of him, addressed with the heel of his club, the left foot forward, the right drawn far back, and his hands at the bottom of the leather. He was not always an accurate driver, perhaps because he had other outdoor interests and would come back to the links in imperfect practice; but his mastery of every kind of approaching shot, cultivated on the short North Berwick

JOHN BALL, JUNIOR
Finish with driver

course, never deserted him, and he was a fine putter in an insinuating manner peculiarly his own, wherein the ball slowed down, hesitated, hovered and then fell in at last. No man was ever better justified in saying —the expression became proverbial among his friends—"We must trust to a pitch and a putt."

Of the first ten Amateur Championships those three players won eight between them, John Ball having the lion's share; but meanwhile there had arisen two other challengers, some seven years younger, most terrible and famous. In 1869 Harold Hilton was born and in the early days of 1870 F. G. Tait, and till Tait was killed in the South African War, their names were constantly bracketed together and their clashes had the added spice,

35

for their respective supporters, of strong international feeling. Freddie Tait was the idol of the Scottish crowd and when he and Hilton met it had much to gladden its heart, for there was one man against whom Hilton could never play, and there was one man against whom Tait could be trusted to give of his triumphant best. Freddie Tait was essentially a match player rejoicing in single combat, lacking something of the machine-like precision that makes for supreme success in scoring but having, combined with a gay and gallant demeanour, the formidable qualities of a killer. He was never beaten till the last putt was holed and his great recuperative powers and his cheerful belief in his own star gave him the reputation of being a lucky player. He was certainly an illustration of fortune favouring the brave, but because he could bring off prodigious recoveries I think those who never saw him have misconceived his game. Such epithets as "slashing" are to my mind inappropriate. They do no justice to the drowsy ease of his swing and the control under which he kept his strength. He could make wild shots, possibly owing to his curious underhand grip of the right hand but not to any reckless *abandon*. On his best days, when no recoveries were needed, it would have been difficult to imagine anyone playing more smoothly and easily and more "within himself."

It would not be fair to set down Hilton as purely a score player. He had not Tait's joy of battle but against any but that one adversary he could fight dourly if always a little anxiously, and though when he was in his prime he let the Amateur Championship regularly escape him he won it four times in the end. Still his greatest achievements were in scoring; two Open Championships won and two more that were only just lost, one by a single and most disastrous error and one, as I perhaps not quite impartially think, by sheer bad luck. At his best he could as nearly put the ball where he liked as any player that ever lived. This accuracy was not that of unambitious steadiness but of a complete and varied mastery, gained by the application of a keen brain to one subject and hours of happy toil in practising. He knew golf through and through and not only his own game but everyone else's; his mind seemed an endless picture gallery of all those he had watched. In combined powers of observation and memory and in unflagging enjoyment of study he had never been equalled.

The two were not only keen rivals of each other, but of their elders. These last, once the pair had come to full maturity, they unmistakably surpassed, save for one, John Ball. Ball and Hilton did not meet very often on great occasions; they seemed to steer clear of one another, but when they did meet I think the influence of old Hoylake days, in which one had been a Champion and the other an aspiring schoolboy, still had its effect. Ball and Tait made the more obvious pair of fighting-cocks and the final of 1899 at Prestwick, which the Englishman won at the thirty-seventh hole, was the greatest of several encounters between the two and one of the classic finals.

CYRIL TOLLEY PLAYING IN THE PRESIDENT'S PUTTER AT RYE
Tee shot at short hole

And now there come on the scene another great couple, again some seven years younger, Robert Maxwell and Jack Graham, both Scotsmen this time, though Graham was by upbringing a wholly English golfer, the third of the Hoylake trinity. Here was a player of unquestioned genius who never won a Championship and never even reached the final. The quality of the game that was in him was beyond question, but he could never quite do it, and the passionate longing of his friends that he should do it, made it all the harder for him. It was often said that had he been accustomed to play golf for several days running, he would not have tired towards the end; but I think the cause lay deeper. He was a fine all-round game player and did

37

A. H. PADGHAM
Playing from a bunker

not lack either vigour or courage but he did lack the love of big and public
fights, "the trampling and the hum" of the crowd. An old coat super-
imposed on his town clothes, a pipe in his mouth, two or three clubs under
his arm, a pocketful of old balls and a summer evening at Hoylake, that I
believe was his notion of golfing happiness, and he played in a Championship with a sad-eyed loyalty to his family and his friends and not because
he wanted to.

For that matter Maxwell was also by instinct a private rather than a
public golfer. He succeeded to Freddie Tait's position as the leader of
Scottish golf but the crowd, much as they admired him, hardly took him to
their hearts as they had his predecessor; the one had rejoiced in the crowd
and the other, as I suspect, in the depths of his being hated it. Maxwell
won two Championships, both at Muirfield, where he was as nearly as
might be invincible. He might well have won elsewhere for he was a
formidable and tremendous golfer. A beautiful player he was not, save for
that beauty that is inherent in any action supremely well done. But he was

JAMES BRUEN
Bunkered before the twelfth green, Birkdale

very strong, capable of an almost mechanical accuracy for round after round, and with it he had a delicacy of touch—the onlooker would not at first have suspected it—which gave its name among his friends to "Bobby's pussycat shot." After the first war he retired not ungratefully into private life and the modern golfer knows him only as a name. It had been one "at which the world grew pale."

Another player of much the same vintage in point of years was James Robb, a member of the St. Andrews Club, which had for years produced a series of fine artisan golfers, such as Laurence Auchterlomie and Willie Greig. Robb was the exception to prove the rule that members of artisan clubs do not do themselves full justice, for he won one Championship and was twice runner-up. He had rather a short quick swing, not at all typical of his native links, and a long game of no great power, but he was a good and courageous match player and a really beautiful putter. His name is not often mentioned among those of the outstanding putters of history but there it surely ought to be and high on the list.

The long break of the war made a more striking difference in amateur than it did in professional golf, for the leading figures of the post-war period had not been known before it. This is not wholly true, for such fine golfers as Robert Harris and Michael Scott won their Championships after the war although entirely mature before it; but the three names that were oftenest on men's tongues were new ones—Wethered, Tolley, and Holderness. Holderness, it is true, had played for Oxford before the war but only now attained to his full stature as a player. The other two burst on the world entirely afresh.

Holderness was in the nature of a pre-war player, in the sense that though strong and wiry and long enough for all practical purposes, his great merit lay in straightness and accuracy; he might have been brought up at Hoylake under the critical eye of John Ball. The other two were rather the advance guard of a new school, gifted with a power hardly dreamed of before, save in the case of such a unique phenomenon as Edward Blackwell, but liable now and then to hit the ball not only extremely far but, for no ascertainable reason, extremely crooked.

This combination of immense length with occasional eccentricity is one that older golfers can never wholly explain to their satisfaction. It may arise from no more recondite cause than that the younger generation follow Edward Ray's advice to one who craved for greater length, "Hit it a —— sight harder, mate." Whatever the reason, it produced in these two new-comers two golfers who could be quite crushingly brilliant but did not always live up to their immense possibilities.

That Cyril Tolley should ever drive crooked seemed incredible and un-necessary, so smooth and round and beautiful was his swing. It was easier to find a reason in Roger Wethered's case. He was a really grand iron player, having a "power of cue," if the phrase be permissible, seldom equalled, but he appeared to apply the principles of iron play to his wooden clubs and this led occasionally to erratic bouts of driving. Perhaps this was a merciful dispensation for had he driven consistently well who could have withstood him? Judged at their best—and Wethered tied for the Open Championship while Tolley twice beat strong professional fields in the French Open—these two had a game in them which very few of our amateurs have ever equalled.

There were other very good golfers to follow: Willie Hunter the Amateur Champion of 1927 and T. P. Perkins Champion of 1928, a product of the strong Midland school, both of whom became professionals in America and so were lost to us. Hector Thomson, also now a professional, was a beautiful golfer and another Scot, Jack McLean, though he could not win the Amateur Championship, won everything in Scotland and came within a putt of the American Championship. Dr. Tweddell, the Hartley brothers and the Irishman John Burke were unquestionably good and yet all these fine players belong to a period of natural depression in the amateur world; the

By courtesy of the Royal Liverpool Golf Club

THE LINKS OF THE ROYAL LIVERPOOL GOLF CLUB
Oil painting by T. Chaulms, 1889

HAROLD HILTON
Oil painting by R. Jack, 1913

American amateurs were better still and for years an American terror stalked our links.

An American amateur team came to Hoylake in 1922 and played an unofficial international. That some of them such as Ouimet and Evans and the then legendary Bobby Jones were greatly to be feared everyone knew or ought to have known, but alas! for that rash scribe who described the rest of the team as no more than respectable scratch golfers. He knew better a day or two later when our team was not only beaten but crushed. After that the Walker Cup was instituted and in the following year a team went from here to play the first match in America. It met what I believe to have been the finest team of amateurs that ever played. Our team came home, in the British view, with their tails between their legs but, in their own view, having done fully as well as could have been expected of them in the other fellow's country; they had won one foursome out of four and three singles out of eight.

Whatever the precise merits of their achievement, it appeared bright by comparison with that of some of their successors. In 1923 against a perceptibly less strong American side our men seemed sure to win at St. Andrews and were robbed by a magnificent collective spurt by their opponents. After that came utter darkness. Wherever the match was played the result was an overwhelming and disastrous defeat. Finally at Pine Valley the score of our side was "as blank as their faces." The American sides were not only very, very good but they played their best on the day as certainly as ours utterly failed to do themselves justice. I have neither heart nor space to tell the story in detail but will jump to the happy ending in 1938.

A great effort was made in that year: there was a clean sweep made of the old selectors; a trial match was instituted—and we won. This turning of the tide synchronised with the appearance of a truly remarkable golfer from Ireland, James Bruen. He was then little more than a schoolboy but the golf he played in the trial matches at St. Andrews, in which he showed himself capable of 69 or so whenever he pleased, was in the nature of a revelation and put new heart into our amateur ranks; he was the architect of victory. In our side was another fine new player, Alex Kyle, destined to be our last Amateur Champion before the war, and all our team, putting on one side their ancient terrors, quitted themselves like men.

That match seems dim and almost trivial to-day after the years that succeeded it, and there is nothing as yet to show the standard of our amateur golf, nor how long and painful may be the climb before it can get back to the glories of St. Andrews in 1938. But nothing can rob us of that memory nor have we any right to doubt that in time there will arise a new race of amateurs worthy not only of their immediate predecessors but of a more distant and equally heroic past.

THE LADIES

"THE Club resolve to present by subscription a new Creel and Shawl to the best female golfer who plays on the annual occasion on 1st Jan. next, old style (12th Jan. new) to be intimated to the Fish Ladies by the Officer of the Club.

Two of the best Barcelona silk handkerchiefs to be added to the above premium of the Creel. ALEX G. HUNTER, C."

So runs the minute of the Musselburgh Club dated the 14th December 1810, which as far as we know represents the dawning of ladies' golf. The name of the Champion Fish Lady is lost for ever and for eighty-three years there is little further word of the ladies in golfing history. True in 1890 the first edition of the *Badminton* volume contained some remarks on the subject by Lord Wellwood under the facetious title of "Women's Rights." Their trend may be sufficiently indicated by a single quotation: "We venture to suggest seventy or eighty yards as the average limit of a drive advisedly; not because we doubt a lady's power to make a longer drive, but because that cannot well be done without raising the club above the shoulder. Now, we do not presume to dictate, but we must observe that the posture and gesture required for a full swing are not particularly graceful when the player is clad in female dress."

Those fatuous observations were disproved in 1893 by the institution of the Ladies' Championship and the first of the three victories of one of the great lady golfers, Lady Margaret Scott, whose swing was by common consent a model of grace. In that year was also founded the Ladies' Golf Union with Miss Issette Pearson, afterwards Mrs. Miller, as its honorary secretary. She was the mainspring and driving power of the machine and so remained for many years. I well remember, I suppose about 1908 or 1909, a journalist who wrote chiefly of ladies' games, exclaiming to me in heartfelt tones, "Miss Pearson is as despotic as the Tsar of Russia." I imagine that she had a resolute will of her own but there is no doubt that ladies' golf owes her an immense debt of gratitude. The Ladies' Golf Union has been a most efficient institution and everything it undertakes is done well. I have an irreverent theory that women like being mildly dragooned better than men do, and from its earliest days the L.G.U. was inclined to what in these days of freedom and democracy we call "controls." It is noteworthy that one of its first objects announced was "To establish a uniform system of handicapping" and this it did with the utmost thoroughness and much sending in of cards. Since then the Unions with their systems of scratch scores for courses have followed faint and pursuing in the ladies' footsteps and I am far from saying they are wrong: only—and I grow old-fashioned—that we seemed to get along tolerably well in our unconverted state.

THE WESTWARD HO! LADIES' GOLF CLUB AT BIDEFORD, DEVON
Drawing from the *Graphic*, 1873

However, I am wandering and must go back to 1893 and the first Ladies' Championship on the ladies' links of the Lytham and St. Anne's Club. There were thirty-eight players, from England, from Ireland, from France but as yet no single one from Scotland. The tournament was a considerable success save in this fact, that Lady Margaret Scott won with too great, indeed with almost ridiculous ease: she had "breathed golf into her growing frame"; she had a course round her father's house at Stowell and had played constantly with brothers, already good and destined to be famous players. She was in a totally different class to all the rest.

So she remained for the next two years at Littlestone and Portrush respectively and then sated with triumph she retired and never played in public again. Curiously enough it was after this then unique figure had vanished that ladies' golf made a great step forward in popular interest. In 1896 the Championship was played at Hoylake and for the first time great crowds assembled to watch it. The winner was Miss Pascoe, a gallant and determined fighter and a good putter, but essentially a made player, without the dash and power or the "fine insolent carelessness" of those who had played from early girlhood. The turn of these ladies teethed on a club was soon to come again, however; Lady Margaret was to have worthy successors.

43

MISS CECIL LEITCH, 1908
Finish of a full drive

A few Scottish ladies had now begun to enter and in 1897 the Championship was played for the first time in Scotland at Gullane. I remember that for a year or two before, I had heard of the three Miss Orrs of North Berwick, that if they would play, the Championship was a foregone conclusion. They came and they played; all three reached the last eight and two met in the final. They had given their proofs; like meteors they flashed across the golfing sky and like meteors expired. They never played in a Championship again and as of Lady Margaret I must say that alas! I never saw them.

The next few years saw the reigns of two very fine Irish golfers from Portrush, Miss Rhona Adair (afterwards Mrs. Cutheell) and Miss May Hezlet (afterwards Mrs. Ross), one of three sisters and a brother all in the front rank. Miss Adair won twice in 1900 and 1903 and lost in the final in 1901. Miss Hezlet won in 1902 and 1907. After them came a good Scottish player, Miss Dorothy Campbell (later Mrs. Hurd) who won twice here in 1909 and 1911 and in America, which later became her home, in 1909 and 1910 and after a long interval in 1924. This is a remarkable record both in the number of her victories and the length of time for which she retained her game.

Meanwhile the Championship of 1908 was not merely a portent as being the first to be played at St. Andrews. It saw the first appearance of one of the two outstanding figures in the history of ladies' golf, a young lady with her hair down her back, from Silloth, the only eighteen-hole course on which she had ever played before. Miss Cecil Leitch did not quite win for she lost at the home hole to the ultimate winner, Miss Titterton, in the semi-final, but she brought into ladies' golf not only a dominating personality but, I think, a more masculine game than had ever been played before by one of her sex. Her wide stance with the ball far away from her, the strong palm grip, the "punch" and vigour of her shots, especially with iron

44

clubs, had something of essential virility that had never been seen. She did not win her first Championship till six years later but from that moment at St. Andrews she was the star which at any rate in public estimation shone with a peculiar lustre of its own in the ladies' firmament.

She did not win, partly, I suppose, because she was still very young; her first essay had been an enjoyable adventure whereas after it she carried the burden of a reputation. Furthermore she had some very dangerous rivals, fine golfers and not to be overawed. The Championship at Hunstanton in 1914 in which Miss Leitch at length broke through, was the first I ever saw and it made me a fervent admirer of ladies' golf ever afterwards. Among the players were four who by common consent stood out: Miss Leitch herself, Miss Ravenscroft, Miss Dodd, and Miss Grant Suttie, and the other three had all won while she still remained an uncrowned queen. Miss Grant Suttie had won in 1910. She was a pro-

MISS RHONA ADAIR
Finish of a full drive

duct of North Berwick, not gifted with any vast length, but a most skilful player with a variety of shots, a resolute determination and a heart-breaking power of recovery. Miss Ravenscroft had great physical advantages, plenty of power, a good free swing and a cheerfulness of disposition which, save when occasionally it overcame all attempts at seriousness, concealed a good fighting temperament. Miss Dodd very slight and light, with a really beautiful style, lacked only a little more of size and strength "to be," as Borrow wrote of Tom Belcher, "I won't say what!" Miss Leitch won but only after once or twice throwing away a winning advantage in a perilous manner. Still win she did and but for the war she must, I think, have reigned not undisputed or unchallenged but clearly pre-eminent for the next few years.

As it was she was as dominating as ever when golf began again and won for the first two years after the war; but now a rival was at hand; the time

45

MISS PAM BARTON, 1936
Finish of a full drive

of Miss Joyce Wethered was almost come. In 1920 had come the first definite threat when in the final of the English Championship at Sheringham she had beaten Miss Leitch by 2 and 1 after being six down with sixteen to play. That, however gallant, was perhaps a rather lucky victory, and Miss Leitch put things to rights next year when they met in the final of the Ladies' Championship at Turnberry. But the challenge was now too insistent to be much longer staved off. They met again in 1922 at Princes, Sandwich, when Miss Wethered won by 7 and 5 and from that day onwards the sceptre had definitely changed hands. Miss Doris Chambers won in 1923, and then Miss Wethered won twice again. The second of these last two years at Troon produced the greatest of all finals between her and Miss Leitch, who came right back to her best game on the right day and only succumbed on the thirty-seventh green. Never was there a more deservedly halved match, never was the necessity for that additional hole so universally regretted. For three years, in one of which Miss Leitch won for the fourth time, Miss Wethered stayed in her tent, but in 1929 St. Andrews tempted her once more into the arena. Again she won, though only after a terrific struggle with a fine American player, Miss Glenna Collett, in which she was at one time five down.

After that she was seen no more except in the Worplesdon Mixed Foursomes, in which for years she showed a power of dragging almost any partner through to victory by the scruff of his neck. She had fully the power of any other lady either before or after her and to that she added a deadly uniformity of accuracy only to be found among two or three of the very best men. Whatever other stars may arise one thing is certain; those who saw this truly great golfer in her prime will never admit comparisons, but will say with pardonable prejudice, "Ah, but you never saw Miss Wethered."

When she and Miss Leitch played no more, ladies' golf suffered not indeed from an eclipse, but from a decline in general and excited interest. This was inevitable but it was in a measure at least unjust to a number of fine players. Miss Enid Wilson, strong, determined, infinitely painstaking, with a real Champion's capacity for playing as well as she had to do in any given match, won for three years in succession and might have gone on winning had she not retired in the heyday of youth and success. Miss Diana Fishwick, still very young, struck a great blow for her country when it seemed that nothing could prevent Miss Collett from taking the cup to America. Miss Wanda Morgan, Miss Jessie Anderson and in particular Mrs. Holm were notable players. There was one, however, who seized the popular imagination and seemed to have recaptured something of Miss Leitch's mantle. This was Miss Pam Barton, whose death on active service during the war was a loss not merely to golf but to all who like friendliness and modesty and simplicity. As in Miss Leitch's case there was something conspicuously masculine in her game. She had to endure the fierce light that beats upon an illustrious "flapper." For three years running she was in the final and at the third attempt she too "broke through" and then, crossing the Atlantic a lone challenger,

LADY HEATHCOAT-AMORY (JOYCE WETHERED), 1938
Finish of a full drive

47

won the United States Championship. After that she seemed to fall off a little but re-established her fame by winning in the last year before the war and there sadly the story ends.

Ladies' Golf has made immense strides since that first meeting at St. Anne's, in particular in the greatly increased power of the players. This may partly be due, though these things are a mystery, to the garments in which ladies now play, so infinitely better adapted to the purpose. It is certainly due to the fact that more and more girls learn the game as small boys do and thus acquire a freedom of stroke rarely given to the late learner.

Not only have ladies become relatively long drivers; they are good all-round wooden club players, accurate and trustworthy. They have to play many more brassy shots than men do, and that is, I am inclined to think, the strongest part of their game. Save in a few cases, it is certainly better than their iron play, for which as a rule they lack something of the required "punch." They are essentially swingers rather than hitters and that is a virtue, but a virtue subject to some inherent weaknesses. It would be natural to assume that on the green, where strength is of no importance and delicacy of touch a valuable gift, the ladies are man's equals if not his superiors, but experience shows this assumption to be fallacious. I am sorry to end even on that mildly ungallant note, for the lady golfers have no more devoted admirer. How the winner of the Creel and the Barcelona handkerchief would open her eyes if she could see them!

SHORT BIBLIOGRAPHY

Golf: A Royal and Ancient Game, 1899, by R. Clark.—*Golf*, by Horace Hutchinson, with contributions by Lord Wellwood and others. The Badminton Library, edited by the Duke of Beaufort. Latest edition, 1902.— *Life of Tom Morris*, 1907, by W. W. Tullock. W. Laurie.—*Fifty Years of Golf*, 1919, by Horace Hutchinson. Country Life.—*My Golfing Life*, 1933, by Harry Vardon. Hutchinson.—*Golf*, 1937, by Henry Longhurst. J. M. Dent.—*Golf: My Life's Work*, 1943, by J. H. Taylor. Cape.—*Golf Between Two Wars*, 1944, by Bernard Darwin. Chatto and Windus